WAVE
PULSE

WAVE PULSE

MICHAEL ZUCARO

atmosphere press

Published by Atmosphere Press

Cover design by Ronaldo Alves

atmospherepress.com

CONTENTS

EYE ON LOVE

ANTERIOR

headlong each avatar
having sought her fragrance
as the gazelle with taut arched
throat bounds across shimmering veldt
as the name whose syllables
he could almost recall
within the tentacles of sleep
throughout the night, then
casting found gem-like stones
across the eddying river, questing
in the mazed streets near
her sun-strewn terrace
whispering across wide waters
to echo balmed keynotes
within the whorls of
her ear

7.30.1972, 9.29.2020
© 2021

3

the ring and meaning
of your word so
often lies
secret from me
I cannot absorb
when you punctuate
it at me and thereby
happens that your
soul arcs on that
word like — I don't
RELATE to you —
and we recoil
in the void like
proton planets
when ages hence
the meaning's revealed
in its arcaneity
the marrow unveils
your tidal sway
except you've ebbed
our next conjunction
light years
awry

CHARISMA AND THE COMMON MAN

'the way they wear their
flesh' you'd think they
owned it and how
they sling their flaunts
be a slight to behold
smack in the teeth of
time's (tee) totallers
oh the tiles fly off
the tinder rekindles
the dead palms flame by the moon
winds gutter as nightriders queue
up while the molls run away with the
goons
but radio got soul
stay tuned

SENTIENT COGNIZANT

so
what that all
the agonies of the sentient
cognizant beings on this
sphere are but a
thimbleful to the
cosmos, all the radiance of
a superstar in
heat can't hold a
candle to that
gleam in your
nuclear focused eye

1.3.1979
© 2012

IN TAMALPAIS LEE

loving nature so
badly you
ache to see her flow
down the drain so
you wait on destiny
mark time as a clerk to
be discovered in
carnival Sausalito
where he'll be rich
and get you with sails
and wheels then wings over
lands enclaved from the press
of the mob, and you'll vow in the
whorls and well-
springs of your inner-
most heart you
love him
too

10.19.71
7.3.90
9.22.99
© 2012

AIRBRUSHED DIVA

flawless, affectless,
free, monochrome in her
select chill beauty
buff airbrushed
porcelain façade pore-
less, auto-exempt from
societal restraint, eluding
nuance and shading of
emotion, irrelevant empathy

having scorned men's flawed
overtures like an avenging angel
aloof, free to bluff
the nothing without,
within she flies

if only
desire would
atrophy with
its will to
revive

7.13.1968
10.23.2010
© 2021

YOUR REFLECTION IN DRAINED CUPS

the owl has taken to
mirror through the
weft the feathers adrift
the floorboard warps and
sways my feet
the rain blew we
hoped it was the
wind as water seeped under
the door this morning your
bare feet in the mud
all vision being suspect
perhaps the replay of late
late shows and cinemas half slept
if earth spy no beauty life lie
bled of its trance
landscapes fade then vanish
one day perhaps crystallized
in autumn rain
they burst in
stillness of eye again

© 2012

ALTAMIRA BY FIRELIGHT

cavern of chthonic springs
the bounding line of
mindseye on bison at spearpoint
chiseled to stone womb
leaps in bound thunder
kinetic as
candle flame flicker from your
eye to mine love
bound in belly and song
Altamira: a view of the high

© 2012

beauty radiates
from her every pore
from each fling of limb through
lambent airs as it
oscillates across the waves
yet to
revivify worth to brush
the strings, across distances
of her encased heart, words as they
are — though images, reverberant
notes in cadence — not quite
vivid to her, find
means of response to the
systole diastole whorls of
her core anima

FOR HURRICANE KALI

random winds tonight drive
us to separate corners
the astringencies rise to
rasp through our voices
broaching no climax we know
the various improvs we might
probe the plot no longer impels

if I don't actively
protest it means
I agree with what
you say
said she

in your dream the crumbled
tower enfolds
in mine the word out of
earshot reverbs

tossing each
other words like Ming
vases eyes trained
on other's face from
avert heads

her eyes run liquid
to indigo skies in
winter bare
nerves lightn–
ing pulse arc stars
she constellates one's
neon desire

descant
shuga pop be
gat tiddly wink the
porsche
bucks high bods reply
old man bundle blind
man bluff

corrugate bodies'
contents: merchant
ice, accordion into
interstellarctic
stills their
music toppling
flat
a trifle

merely objective
you're being merely objective
the presence of the observer
alters the condition of
         the observed
don't
         look at
me as I
         speak she re-
verbs

2.16.2015
8.22.2018

NOCTURNE CONSTITUTIONAL

night, sleep will
none of me,
a fit of dream pitches me in
flight to pulses irridescing color
across the black, the window
wide to rain, your
body slung in abandon beside
me, what images ride your
being across what amber fields
buoying your molten core
simmering volcanically, reeling mine

this moment unique
catenation of
chance elements
chanced faces
kaleidoscopically
slipping together

and away
this brain
same torpor
this moment
as the last
sensibility must be
sliding
inert to
catenate
gradation of stupor
with this snowflake
instant

One Hundred Tenth and Fifth
crystalline murk obliterates
retinal reception
vertical hold describes
720 degree arc
and screen floods
a million grey
flickers of
murk crystal

phenomenology can't wait
on epistemology the pearl
gull mused on swells of
gelid sky

DETONATE

the tighter our fusion
the wider the mind
explodes its antique
fixtures musty
drawing rooms
black hole yawn
across the faces of aeons
black gap between your
face and mine
black rush the cosmos
speed of no light
involution yet
if only through marrow
would echo
melody to beguile
the hour of its acid
bite I'd bide the
sweep of broader
currents to farthest
reaches of spectral light

7.13.75
1.28.76
© 2012

PRIME CUT

this instant
unique
concatenation of
chance elements
chance faces
kaleidoscopically
slipping together
then awry
brain reverts to
same torpor
this moment
as the last
sensibility slides
unable to
catenate
gradation of apathy
with this snowflake
drift

© 2012

MONEY GALORE

YIN AND YANK

ye sharks and pikers
jimmy statistics
juggle them books
shim them sham
gimcracks simulate
treason
reason bread 'n circus
neospeak newsprint
doublethink
bojangle shuck 'n
jive softshoe routines
though sun dream
infinite wave long
artery and vein

MOEBIUS EPISTEMOLOGIES

not into dissertational
striving to prove or
lock in analogies
financial formulae
econometric theorems
papal bulls ex cathedra
formulaic investment
derivatives prefixed to
future's indeterminacy
not ignoring PR's sway
ah, robotize to
"The Half
Life of Facts"
perhaps might
fudge the curious
recurrence of archetype and
analogy
hey, Pi be infinity
corporate universified
the individue dispensable
aligning soul trajectories into
oops collisions, but
hey calculus got
soul, no?

10.12.2012
© 2012

ON THE VERGE

after surprising incursions and
unveilings of executive machina-
tions how very balming the
contemplation of sudden
intestinal detonation of
mute stone bastions
once corporate callous
burst of a boil
sublimely soothing the
leisured lift the
cinematic slow
drift of items of
progress the
whitewall tires steam
irons the no-
return bottles
pried from coagulation
by volcanic
bellow so
NASA taught us
peaceful to witness
esthetic distance the
lever

SATURNALE

chorale of Magritte mustachioed
  black bowlered brokers
shouldering jagged broomsticks and
  pumping forelegs in rockette
rhythms left then right
  across the screen of drawn lids

boldface neon numbers
  multiply swell contract

silkwhite thighs dilate
  then snapback the mandibles:
lacquered chop sticks in
  bejewelled puff fingers
of the Caliphs of Braaz

© 2012

AFTER ROBERT CREELEY

the poor contort their
bones round gears and sprung
machines of obsolescence
while reborn
bourzhies avert their
olfactories and chortling think
they're crazy

© 2012

DERIVATIVE TREMENS
to the Duke and Dauphin

arms akimbo legs
awry the supply slide curves as
funding fathers' delirium roils
at the scorn-cold wrath o' green theory
spin green globular
green spends the globe
as junk bondage speeds round
the end run, as made off
unchained lords of obfuscation
equivocate on the make
banks too big to go big bang
so trust we go bank the bigger
no bust, or bank on
in perpetuity war

commoditize passion
commodify compassion
any way you
dice it serve it up
cold so check balances
cashiered with
prejudice in extremis how
greed be god
oh laissez-faire
disdaining any rein of
regulation research
on rationale

off the record?
it's leveraged
we're maxed
the check's in the mail
tween you and me don't
cash it 'til
Moonday next a
flack fax o' facs
when the tire hits
the road, when
the facs don't fit

the specs,
bend 'em round
the last laugh curve

laissez-faire buyer be
ware

LEGAL TENDER

man in a mirror
man in a lake
man off top of the head
reeling forth his line
man in a sky strafed with
ricochet riddles

jump
cut jigsaw
switch flip
cirquit cohere
to image re-
verb then
blink pixels
awry to shard spun
in wave run
counter cross
current rip tide
bent back swan
dive

proceed by opposites
advance with indirection
bred by years of
deliberation and perspicacity
leap backwards three
times blinking alternate
eyes
describe an arc embracing
all that you see in
no uncertain
terms

2.12.2015
© 2020

FOURTH ESTATE, INC.

hackers scan fax of skimped facs
from corp-grant-tied sci ops,
market re-skewers and their
flacks to dish to the
duped, fleeced, flummoxed,
thus corpus media
advertease ya

fax flips facts
pitch hacks the latest
spin to dish
to the sacked

corporate enumeration
corporeal numb the nation
digit alienation
ex-senators de-mask to
corporate shills,
astro-economical corporatocracy
kowtow in line
hierarchy in session,
grey malevolencies:
nothing personal
just your banal non-entity
merits a number
now, oops, obsolete

that they'd clone us
rezone us
ozone-hole us
eighty-six us
nix, fixate,
renix us
dish our licks,
crises, non-anomalies
to us is a given,
data, news

life a
miracle whose

banality bores into
pavement til say
hacks, flacks, and hash artistes
sow in fields of flack

dumb down nation
0, digitize, standardize,
penalize, sterilize,
amortize the
vested and vaunting
laissez gerrymandangling
their billions not – off course —
to the minions, yet

obtused, obfusced
obnoxed, aflush with hype
shall we adulate your laissez-
faire oil-glut evictories
in corporate skirmishes to
taxation without representation
inflation without cessation
citizens united behind
the 1%, or extradited,
trickle down to your
laid-off, mort-gaged, spewn
counting coup
corpse mounds
statistics of dread, of body count,
stacking your masses huddled in
hopes foundered

y'all opine? ya
sure to whine
hey, it all depends on the spin you're
dished, on the buzz you're fed,
something you can stick your finger on,
really bite into, ya know
flack fax o' facs
when the tire hits
the hacked-up road, when
the facs don't fit
the specs,

bend 'em raw,
stay tuned

11.17.2019
© 2020

ART THRIVE

AFTER PAUL KLEE'S
MYSTICAL CITY SCENE

on drifting up Laurel to
Xanthippe's on the balm of a Santa
Cruz night and passing the liquor
store whose amber light spills out the
yawn door, ruminating on the strokes of
history in California making
it in the back
seat of a '56
Chevy or so and think-
ing what's it to
do with the raga
drone of its crystalline
spheres, the bow across catgut
and is it
Jupiter ignites across aeons to counter-
point this gabled Victorian
rooftop shamble secure oh
pure domesti city in the corner of my
eye this funk this
making and re-instigating
as passing a dim
back alley where a tan
bitch lollsplays as her old
black mastiff lets bark a
phlegmatic few at the
philosofarce
of this trespass

© 2012

N.Y. BARDO

You are suspended in a
state of total recall of
your life you are
rooted in a movietheater
where the projectionist
feels the exact moment
you squirm to
evade and he replays it
as often as necessary
you are bound in
reels of endless speculation of
alternatives edited in the
heat of that moment past
until you recognize the
rays and the flashes and the
fury as nothing as
emanations of the
waves of your febrile
brain
       what then
you stand up
the audience walked out
after the first scenes
you see
your hands in your pockets
your life a
strew of celluloid on a
gritty floor
a billion frames strangely
       connected
you wait twenty-five minutes
to stand on a bus

© 2012

AT THE MODERN

the painting had the look of
one observed
the guard had the surreptitious
look of one about to
observe the shufflers and cogno-
scenti had the
look

the city brooded and
bred the rain relieved
the clouds to grease the
rust interstices of motley façades
the wide bay window had the
look of one boring through
the city

his back avert the
pane dissolved

the camera at home
thus unhanded he hung
as one brooding the refinement of
sensibility

© 2012

AFTER PAUL KLEE, THE COLTRANES, MAHAVISHNU JOHN

time and again
oh but
if never later
then now
why 'and again'
time forever
impedes
when if
idylls perdure
ever and
all
ways just
in time

© 2012
9.28.2020

PROJECTIONIST'S FAIR SHADOW

she wants to scream
but dreams not why
dares the wind cast
her last die
tears her hair
peels her eye
wants to dream
dreamt she'd fly
once the wind
drowned voice in
sky wants to
dream her, knows
not why

with thanks to Robert Duncan for
his lines singing
"The Truth and Life of
Myth", the spontaneous
patterning the iron
filing of
daily conversings, random
meetings around odd corners,
catenations in the grasp and
clutch of lines half-
recalled a year on the
road without script
reverberating yet
vibrantly

ON KLEE'S
GROUP INTERLACED

line feed
fast draw
hand as
quick the
eye fore-
cast what
will to be
come

8.10.74
© 2012

FROM A PHOTO OF A HOPI PRIEST
BY ADAM CLARK VROMAN

seedjar spills into night
snake priest jaws gripped
eyes glisten
paint smears the cheeks and
breast in white fingered on dusk
skin
what spells your stillness
as pinpricks of star
stream re-
flect from your abstract
stare out the left photo
frame

1985
© 2012

DON GENARO TO DON JUAN

for Hunce Voelcker

(aside) to me
cocked yr notebook and
pen? my ears a
quiver my pen, ball-
point, twitching in the faintly
acrid air charged with electric
crackling between the sorcerer and his
crony, a nudge in the ribs
which do we pronounce more
miraculous the Word made
flesh or the compulsions of
flesh wound into word to
spark the gap twixt
mind and mind one
millenium and perhaps the
next which do we declare by
fiat of will most
remarkable
the nudge in the rib
the back leap from one
crag to the higher the
knowledge of one's
ally within the flesh
without word or
twinge of neural pen

10.27.74
© 2012

indigo dusk
the starlings won't fly
into my composition of
rooftops, pine and sundown
mackerel clouds, first gold–
etched then smoke purple
though Rae flutes the "Rites of
Spring" (transcribed) so I
shelve the camera
back at the desk maybe
words unwary will
drift in my net

2.2.76
© 2012

UNIVERSE/
MULTIVERSE

ABOUT TIME

time like a broken
record, needle bores
reverbs of
snores ad infinitum
obsolescing

to dodge in and
out of time
to dodge within
interstices of every-
one's twists, time
bent to make one's own

"(I measure time by how a body sways)."
                        - Theodore Roethke

time churn
chattel fleeced
foam spackle flee
jackknife windsplice
time at the top of the
carton congeals

in raw winter, stripping the
leaves of base-
mented trees, the avocado, grape-
fruit, the jade's shrivelling to ashen
silver before its limbs,
withering in time progenitors'
vitae from our root to
mere reminiscings to hover
insubstantially, lips ripped from
mammalian data
dayadhvam
yet
umbilically yours,
love wends its
wiles, ways in other,
significant or no

to run from place is
to run from time and
again

digit's a metaphor, a linear
construct stacked atop other to
approach limit ever receding
infinitude measures of
which stats
skew the
tower of babble
on while spacetime curls
itself twisting its
moebius insides
out

squaring the circle as
though mastering space
bounding the
uni- (is it?)
verse
by its receding immeasure-
ability as pi
recedes as
my fantasy from
your being ricochets
into fourth
dimension is it that
all potentiality all fantasias
couple as with antimatter to
kaleidoscopic identities
in corposant
being?

dustmote glint off slant light down
like dancer frozen in arc
lights riptide glare

petrified tranches de vie
in Pompeii
persuade anew that all's
been felt in-
tensely before, all lusts, all

percepts of beauty inextricable
from all sorrows at
fleet transience of
things women and
men lungho Via delle Tombe

in the novel, in drama, saturate in
tragedy, the comic yet surfaces as
relief, but the lyric
beyond agon, catharsis
beyond the loss, lotus
petal by petal sheds
express through to denoue
the unknotting into
image on the lyre's
oscillance reverbing like the
photo still phenomena

wishing we could talk about forever
yet in Heraclitus' river of fire change
a cyclicality: variation into theme,
harmonies into melodic
twists la premiere pèche de l'été

the nature of longing's such that
time has up its sleeve
another surprise to
tantalize while
stalking significant form in
the welter of raw
horizon recedes before the eye like
the wellspring of one's dream or
reverberant ripplings on
phantom shores

massive striate stone
leaf upon leaf of accrued
time

each iota being
ruled by time at
each angle of
which adjoin uni-

verses that time
may decline

in the intestinal
tract of language
lies the missing mind-
body link in portenjambe-
manteaux like
moebius curling space/time
word the will dallies with its
personae the sinuous tongue
contrapuntally stoking wavelengths
of phenomena's fluidities with
Morse messages digitized
syncoping pulse

phenomena raw sensa
data distill into
syllable music counterpointing
etymologies
runic reverberances
iotae past recycling
wheeling currents of light
supernova to nebula
congealing to re-star unless
time warps
black hole sucks
light reel to
re-nonentity
or cosmentality

time
space
energy
light spiral
priority
hierarchy or
simultaneity?

4.18.1986
8.22.2018
© 2020

50

jade white
fogged forest meadow
lapis lazuli
interstellar blue

propound nothing
stalk the immanent

lone deer spring
highway to meadow and
river below
our strung cars
beaded red lights
trickle in broad day
to bedrock

in, out this miraging,
diaphanes of vision or light
collude and drift beyond
peripheries of ruminant sight
to uncover luminous seams
crystalline negative space conjures
etched pine needlings in
the dusk indigo sky

11.9.1990
© 2012

NOVA TECH

man on the moon
cancer on the run
tinkering with gene orbits
mortality deferred
myth media rooted
immortality round the
bend, or the next,
is all arriving a
leaving?
who rests
assured that
matter's to rest til
human will move
primally, that
the trigger won't
spark
til the finger
itch that flame
won't burst til
man grunts
go,
yet
in the Crab Nebula mysteries
eyes that would sere
through the film of the world
lungs that would burst through
to ether beyond
ears strain to attune
raga of planets in transit
world, keep your distinctions
let thrive such metaphors

1.24.1984
5.22.2006
© 2012

BANG THEORY RAG
A ROMANCE OF THE PARTICLE AND THE WAVE

"The self persists like a dying star
In sleep, afraid."
— Roethke, "Meditation at Oyster River"

like a pulsar of exploded
desire the nucleus exuding its sway like
musk over its receding nebula,
estranged grits for
congealing of the new star, its
avatar the self perceives its
pneumena luminous project
splat across the starscreen
prana light spins out the eye of
storm winks as

black hole yawn in
face of aeons
black gap athwart your
face and mine
black jaws agape across
cosmos at the speed of
no light to swallow involute
spirit's intestinal tract

So
if it's a corporeal or bailout world
leering over the neon void

there lie you and this landscape
there this raw escarpment of land
embroiled in your somnolent strokes
fathoms below then
you as this land sweat
lava from its pores and fissures of
you draped in ripple flame
fanned across slopes of
smolder by tongues of desire, for
beneath
lie you this lady feverishly

tossing to
carve the empyrian to your fuguing
concavities undulant
drapes inciting the sky to ignite

white dwarf opalesces
blue white absenting
itself from the diadem awhile of
Cassiopeia to swivel
arc spiral
round the triple stud
blade, florescing the nebula in
great O'Ryan's persona
fixed stars blink, flurry into
milky spray

earth scraper lady she
sieve handfuls of loam
fling dragon's teeth in
the stark of the moon
blue lady recline in hollow
abstractions riddled with perforated
desires' ricochet off mirror cloned
omnivore eyes behold
horned toads, winged serpents dive
pterodactyls ply the rancid waves as
twits, crones, wry coun/sellers
cavort, carping damsels in
distressed throes siren to
cyborgs and drones riding
quasars, masers, probing the cobble gloom
recoil to fly in the teeth of the
pock-faced tin pan two-bit moon as the
molls run away with quarks what got charm
nexi in a field charged with joy's positractions
while woman splays in the mindscape over
amber whale hills of Marin
like mammalian dolphins and songwhales
though jackal claw rake at stray
flank of doe arcing, buck
angling off key as the
loam congeal to scrapheap

raw earth cast in concrete
city shrug in spasmodic bucklings along
rifts faults the aeons spell

O "the street giveth and the street taketh
away" —Cat Mother and the Allnight Newsboys
the sun impregnates asphalt
concrete cracks under groans of
spirit strafing the petrific flows with
seed of light

sun wane
earth roll her back
town shut tighter than
Venus fly trap
skull houses grin
auto hypnosis in
the ebb and
flow of my shadow
with radial ghost
echoes under multiple
neon suns
before televisored eyes
bulldozed culture slides
faults rip, Holy Helens erupt
Ahmageddowns helix, elide

woman's backslide into eddies of timescape the
camera in
hand jack reel out
woman's loll in landscape of
stalking eyes like overripe fruit
drawing flies
strafing seed and neuteronics,
tactically

nukes hover erectly over folds
and crannies scaped woman in vision of
flesh within loam pores inscaping

boost slung into orbit
deep thrust into outer

space
fired neutrons to split
atoms, sperm at ova

if they'd blow it for a buck, whim or
fluke of the switch
let dissolve in a flash while
ambling her nooks, crevasses
damp interstices amber
whale mamelons grand tetons
let atoms splay, ganglia smear
across deserts of black,
absence,
translucence?
what color oblivion

the way of the white
cloud, diffusion
diaspora
today like any other except
we weren't waiting
marooned on this timeshoal light
years off your
eyes unblinking past care
hover within my frictive
span arcing

blood warp
time weft
open to night's frictive spheres
umbilus snipped
omphallic orbit about
stellar careers

winnow flesh
translucence warps
film over involute eyes
yet the persistence of form
in the effluvia of
siren sweet images of memory
terra cotta flesh

sea anemone eyes through whose
tendrils dart
sun suffused bank of ocean cumuli
insinuates zygote flagella through
crackpate Rosette nebula
wail in thy tympany

so the nuke's a dud
hot rocks, morning light
scanning the silence of the self
your words tangential
to the etched arabesques
tracking mind how
fluid the skeleton to
taut sleek splendors of
ne plus ultra fox smooth the silk
over feral hip with one
stroke of static while
sunlight through the prism
of blood bares skeletal
architectonics of
mandalic corpuscle[1]
snowflaking wave lady be
wordflesh with
me, dustmote drift in my
own mirrored lights
sophistries ploys putdowns poems
words clot into silence
clear light bloom of the A-
tom flash

mushroom in silence

out of synch, static on the line
the dead dream through
crevices of earth
like buried metaphors
finding ourselves each
worthy of love though
love's left self in the
lurch gasping for light
that won't seep through

such dreams as love's
laid upon

black hole yawns, black
net gapes like a
bat out of phase
black gap dilates and
contracts systole diastole
the heart under
pressure of its own
gravity bank-
rupts, goes
supernova, writhing
phosphorescence into night

what spells the con-
stellarctic auroral splays
what conjure the aeons as
legion Chichen Itzas,
Palenques, Babylons,
Stone Henges swear
to unravel the Rosette
Nebula's mask[2]

to this static
retorts homo eructatio
philosofarcing within the
careering arcs of opalescing orbs
as hot nukes seed dawn's
early warning
flatulencies launching the
spirit in its
flight out its dozing in
interstellarctic lethargies, wise
pearling every
action begetting its chain
redaction ad infinitum linking
the stars somehow by
gaseous politics of the spirit, well

what of the music, the
percosyncopations of bright spheres in

sic transit gloria's
radiant pearl bubblings in what beaker on
whose bunsen burner
what light behind
the pinpricks in
the pitch black plays
wot naught but
what's got
wrought

1978
© 2012

ELISION FIELDS

before elapse to
total eclipse
flip elliptically back to
time elastic

within this granite solidity
a dance of particle/wave
between being and
not

as in
quartet for a unifying
string theory, or is it
music of the
spheres or their cacophony,
take two, via particle
in oscillating
wave counterpointing self to
that elusive other
half

thesis antithesis
synthesis antithesis
syn/anti as
moebius strip

that all knowledge
be tentative
subject to revision
based on subsequent percepts
or discoveries proceed how?
on correlation with internal
predisposition?   based
whither? a gene in DNA
wave

still
tending one's portion of
phenomena and idiom, one's
parsec of earth lodestoning one

out of effluvia meditating as
egret in the rippling
eye on the instant
flicker without blink eliding between
percept and dart

emotion, passion reticulate
striate the sinews
passion slights rebuffs
striate mountain
wind carved
tectonically reshuffled into
avatar
striations, magma-flown
wind-blown, time tracks,
petrific flows, systole
diastole, dialog of wind
and rock
planet ripples, buckles, slides
tectonic plates spindrift, abut, mount, elide
stars luminesce, evanesce, coalesce,
lives loyalties that would
elide, selves abut
tectonically
grate, erupt, implode
to black hole
within

this life or bardo
as conduit to other
lives spins future,
past, as passage,
approaching limit, never
arrives
but veers on
moebiously

no clear
vision
dogma informing, yet hold
relativist sway to
random winds at

bay by what, verisimilitude,
sense, or phenomenological
persistence he'd
never read but a resonance
of imagery to the tuning
fork within strings
without

as cloud transmuting to
wind drift as
self might perdure
adrift in permafrost
of change

5.30.12
© 2012

HUMAN WILL
UNIVERSE

DITHYRAMBICS

beyond thesis antithesis syn-
thesis montage
yin yang sticks, cracks, more
primal than a
locomotive able to
leap like a
deity ram that
which maketh
Zeus hurdle to
beget anew: ditto
rambunctious
dithyramb man
by the rhythm of
song beget his
godship

© 2012

SYZYGIES IN CURVED AIR

the moon the sun
the stars our reach
beyond our grasp
the comet elides our
dreams tantalize
stay tuned for the triad the
hottest since
Kohoutek hang on
til Halley's combust the
new aeon the next
twist of the gyre
be all our imprevisions
beyond their imprecations
now and at the
parsec of our ignition to
incandescence, each photon
gone supernova

© 2012

OF COSMOGENESIS

"universe in a grain of sand"
                    — William Blake

in a universe of multi-
verses whose narrative's more resonant than
reverting of mirrors ad infinitum masking
selves to alter egos each to sole orbit
though ours may elide tangentially once
and cohere perhaps for seasons may-
be eras then elliptical gravitas
pulls each askew for
aeons, avatars

dabbling long
cosmology hypotheses global history
mythology analogy
as derided by digitalists
absolute realists or fabricationists
beyond atom to boson beyond to
uni/multiverses

from geocentric to
heliocentric to
multi-globular verses
while the methane machine
exudes oceans of photons
like stars through earthlings'
microbes iotae of subcon
memory?

atoms protons electrons
neutrons arc, quarks! what
sparks neurons in our veins?
bosons fermions
fandangoing no less?
are Higgs boson and fermion,
irreducible as yet, the
ultimate omnipotentates or
be they transuniversally
interdependent particles waves

interactively yin
yanging ad infinitum

epistemology phenomenology
cosmology theology
demonology monologue
duality trinity
thesis antithesis
synthesis ah
antithesis ad
infinitum contrapuntally
beyond history's
epilogue
hang a left through the
wormhole across
minds of women, men,
traverse in a flash the
architextures of cells and
inter-orb magnetics swaying
in drafts of Leipzig's
St. Thomas, as say J.S.
Bach keying their passion-wrought
permutations of number embodied in
relations, or solitary riffs during
converse with the unwilling
and uninspired transporting to
concourse with prodigious progeny
who abandon his polyphony,
resurfacing centuries
on

do polyphony and counterpoint
infuse both brain lobes
each to emit its own melodic rhythm,
integral yet interweaving, as two
by two, female male
conjoin/isolate
tangentially

analogies between
celestial and terrestrial
bodies, attraction,

repulsion, mutual immersion
if f=XX yet
m=XY two
particles awave in divergent
galaxies light years
remote communit-cate
at will or impulse the well-
tempered composer
inculcating form suffused
with passion distilled in
time whose grains re-weave
dance to gigue, sarabande

wind wave mountain striations
emotions passions all
throb to star's boson
fermion neutrino stream
bursts, attraction repulsion
mutually inherent
in all particles, their anti-s and
beings, aflush in wave
strands in wood, rock, cloud,
rills, ocean wave
as sinews of world
flesh, contortionate to
winds, breath, contingent to
heat, passions of magma
within the core
pebbles in concrete
galaxies in dark
matter stew worm-
holes from one
perspective to moebius
inverse
jump cut from
being to not, back
not then but
while

approaching limit by
half-step boson to fermion
— intime? — ad infinitum or

wormholed into multi-
versed opposite
cell, multiverses
bubbling like
thoughts sentient
incohering these millennia

within bosons, what?
dark matter, iotae or black
naught? approaching constantly
prime particle by
limit, each particle content with
isolate uniquity?
adrift in wave of radiance
through darkness
shuffle the deck, each
parsec awash in oceans of
neutrinos pulsed, hardly
neuter, wild card a-flush

striations of selves, magma-flown,
wind-blown, time tracks,
petrific flows, systole
diastole, dialog of wind
and rock

to know object by
nomenclature's to pin
it within genus,
classification, organ-
ization, but of
beings' interrelations,
interweaves, open eye to
pore, wrinkle striations,
gesture, stance, gaffe
shifting for balance

in selva oscura
in dark of heart
in savage thickets of
selves obscured
ipso snubbed,

or snuffed, by uber-
self, birthrights
snookered, Esau
cast to wild
cosmos dark is
it word that
sparks light
in voice a
part of or spewn
from black
hole maw

calculating arc trajectory of
this word and its angle
of re-entry to your lobes,
one off, its ricochet,
which degree precisely
le juste to
penetrate, permeate,
reverberate long the very
fibers of you is it
plausible ever by
alter intent?

neutrinos flushing through our pores,
sinews, bones drinking ocean waves,
do neutrinos spin neurons to
tango, fandango, or frenzy raw?

whereas matter and anti-matter
co-magnetize across universe
to co-annihilate, neutrinos through
your particles
entwine with neurons in
mine as do
Socratic half-selves
but what of
singularity? if duality undone
at heart
of black hole yet
abhorred by sentients
as vacuum, will it

rush to intrude
upon or within
bubble burst to next universe,
does singularity — or is it
depothesized, for good,
for now? — swallow
duality, even particle and anti-
particle pulverized, aflush into
black hole?
or remnants minced by
singularity worm-
holed into multiverse of
opposite cell (or is it?)
til wormhole
pinballs us back
to flanking black hole or beyond
time mathematically

threads of meaning unravel
frictioned static
charges bounce off
membrane, to fathom an atom
or black hole to
naught, or singularity
or wormhole to
re-scrambled uni-/multi-
verses, next
selves mitose into
doubles, other opting to
occupy same footsteps,
not tangling, yet veering in
string theory intertwine rag

after particle wave systole
diastole diffuse
— conversation's expansion ebbing
into lone meaning estranging,
our voices weaving in polyphony
or colliding contrapuntally? —
contract, is each
or just one deflated via
black hole to

singularity or shredded to
zygote avatar

if flushed into black hole
self ripped from alter
ego, interpersonality reshuffled
dialogue counterpoints to blather
or simultaneous monologues,
i.e, cacophony
into dark matter
cores flushed by
neutrino wave beyond light,
is one spewed into
alternate multiverse or
beyond to singularity
or alter
dreamscape?

GYROSCOPICS

particles dance in waves of becoming
matter isn't, except in its flicker
between being and its
not, like light between two
cells on reeled film, body cell mitoses like
solo godhead, prime particle modulating
into tumors metastasizing to
usurp body organs, body politic reversing
polarity, liberal to conservative, plebes to
patricians, radical self-rightists to
savage, systole
diastole, thesis anti-
thesis synthesis antitheses
gyrate under iron economics in
molten flux, iron corroding, scions squandering
fortunes amassed by buccaneers,
privateers, deprivationists,
self reels
moebiusly, equipoised
in the pivoting still
point within the churning
whorl?

2.7.1996
8.21.2018
© 2020

WAVE PULSE

to Billy lightning struck
the family word over your
illumined demise constricting the core
of this younger child's heart, your
apotheosis to the pantheon of resonant
fears, if the tentacles of the deep
don't clutch at the root, then
one bolt from the bruise-blue chars
memory of your translucent face's charmed
grin plucks chords, so
what the n-thousand
natural melodic
riffs alert to sentient
cognizances are but a
jiggle to the jangling universe,
not all the radiance
of a supernova
in heat holds a candle to that
spark in your fathomless
nuclear eye

1983
© 2012

FREEWAY

cumulus massed high in the
west against the auto's advance
its sweep at eighty
invincible the churn of pistons
through bluff vectors of
wintry gusts
but at its back
fan splayed bursts
apocalyptic light
igniting self-inquiry
in quest for viable goal
within the Gold Coast mode

1973
© 2012

JUMP CUT

lapped
cool waters
breeze across Grand
Tetons and beyond distract
the heat concentric
light, transport us to
landscapes cross prairies
deserts seabeds ancient
reefed in limestone
sandstone
eroded at leisure to
buttes, mesas long familiar as
amber lights disport us
foreground framed against
the aeons' relief
sculpting

8.4.79
© 2012
edited 7.2020

in the teeth of
routine to propel one's
self beyond the husking of flesh
to launch the chrysalid
soul like an ICBM of love ignition
beyond lethargies and
recalcitrances into
interstellarcing orbits,
circulating, associating with
magneto sways and
consciousness, what of?
of wave, its
vibration as message
as music's astral
vibe

3.27.85
© 2012

RESET SEE

to be authentic, press
RESET, insert
THE LOOK disc, press
Enter, follow
directions on
screen scripted
but see, hear,
think, read,
reach, grasp,
recoil,
see deep
within all

11.12.2002
12.10.2004
© 2021

THE GECKO AND THE SKINK
for Robin and Chuck

if time is and lies
in wait upon us
then being
28 cycles or shortly
there, anticipating as
ever contorting the
needles round
time's mock face

as if life were
to perdure in such twists
Lear's buffoon whistles
an out mode
tune on the
crag moors of Kronos

river roll
awake me
from these time-
spanned
nights sprung
loose from days
tolled in coin

river sweep the
seasons through
the vein
river flush this
time tick
out the pulse

the sunlight diffuse
silver etch dustmote drift
zero gravity
the I timeless
from here all art
there emanates no
other eternity

1973
© 2012

82

starts as a droning
winds into chant, wreathing on
gusts, rising on eddies, emerges
as song reiterating each morn
in a dream just before
waking they'd call it
one's power one's
vision of
world within the
folds of earth though soiled,
savaged in coils of soured
desire, blame without measure
measure the time the
treasure the trickle or
veritable plenitudes of
joy pleasure and
pain chrysalids into
prismatic rains of
sound song in touch
brush the pores to unravel
whorled prints of flesh
raw reticent
receptors stark wide
spread to rushes of
white heat harmonics of
corpuscles in the nebula
pneuma throughout the inter-
stellar reaches

5.10.86
© 2012

having never directly heard from
God, yet deepest thanks I often feel
and think to him, for who
alerted this mind's awareness
silently from that snorkeled
swim under waves out
toward the routed freight
ships across Far Rockaway Bay?
Who halted pneumonia then asthma from
blotting my breath? Who
prevented that Atlantic Beach 9-feet wave from
arching my spine to the verge?
Who held my fingers' waning grasp on
that Rocky Mountain cliff? Who else
has sparked such vivid viewpoints my way?
Who feeds me insight throughout life?

3.28.2018
© 2021

PLEISTOCENE DREAM

saber-toothed bones strewn
across stone array
through cavern cores
no dearth of fear

in echoing of divine
silence, to backflip past
virtual orphanics, into colloquies of
adulthood, beyond serial
incompatibilities with other
insular or clustered selves, alter
egos, frères semblables, double entendre,
beyond house-of-card theories bedrocked on
sand, into reverbing memory of
how cities die,
let us count some ways
petrifically, under lava
rills, horrendously, lashed
within hurricane, tsunami blasts,
flotsam, jetsam, ocean swells
into wave, encompassing,
towers imploding
lives, lights

core of cave like the corkscrew
stairs at Pompeii's Villa dei Misteri
out of light two
twists into utter
dark void, then
back climb past stone corpses
rebirthed for life wonderers

3.21.2009
6.18.2020
© 2021

ON LONGS PEAK, ROCKY MOUNTAINS

crevasses, most footholds half-
boot wide, ascent raw, arduous
along its virtually 90° stone wall
a steel rope anchored for
the sheer vertical lift
but not depriving us climbers
the urge to ascend
yet detouring first to a
crest at the left, fingers clutching
the brink of rock
eyes enthralled by the
cobalt blue lake three-
thousand feet below
mirroring the sky, its
beauty amazes as vibrantly
as its challenge, then returning to climb
to the crest that sparks
thrill as its awe as
surrounding boulders well below
wave out to the
horizon surrounding us
but amassed clouds begin to
merge overhead to drip from our sky
we head to mountain's descent side
to discover its 90° peril again
five thousand feet of boots'
half-width on slick wet stone
any slip leading to air, glide, collide
yet miracle exemption from such slide
along stone into oblivion
left to thrive on its eagles' vista

2020
© 2021

SNOW CARVE

the angling of skis lets
one absorb the
concavities convexities
of mountain
swell the earth core
glacier carved to
solar wind
petrific wave
yet

skiing in white-out fog
the contours fade, one
rises and sinks
like a bark foundering in
hurricane swells,
past floods out
future if
it weren't that
will exerts sway

9.24.1983
11.30.2013
© 2021

at South Shore
waves overhead
curved backward
no swandive this
suspension like a particle's
ballast in astral wave
no surf glide
but spine arched back to the limit
with heels flung high then
pitched over shoulders
time in fast forward
as the will to rewind
ebbs
wave slings the body
like a gauntlet onto
taut sand
yet in need to re-thrive

7.1.1984
4.1.1992
© 2021

THERMALS

lofting on thermals and cross-
current winds, sheer
rhythms via counterpoint, later
surfing in wave and undertow,
gliding, pirouetting on swells
in snow, writhing in eddies of
blood and breath, kiting on
currents of thought and desire
the self in polyphony with
other

vying to possess, to fix,
freezes fluidity, ossifies,
shatters, dissolves so that
not desiring breeds despair and
alien festerings, yet
riding on flux, kiting on
wind, releasing breeds tomorrows

remembering, resurrecting beauty
can't go home again in
the Heraclitean river of fire, but
look homeward and in the
revivified deeds past
might one restore the spirits'
voices, faces long faded
where late the sweet vibes rang

4.4.1996
8.27.2020
© 2020

HILLS WAVES GRAINS

these hills sway
waves across the globe
the grains in stone and wood
in flesh in sand
cohere in tides, ocean,
thought as hills grains waves
dreams weave in flux

of undulant line
and resonant
chord, how all
sing, rhythms flow
throughout their veins

wave and cloud drift
sunlight and shade feed
heartbeat, blood throbs

wave within pulse of
all history's lives, which all
must weave worth in marrow
and mind

10.1.2010
8.11.2020
© 2021

your art's sheer
magic as incantation
the words dis-
tract while
rhythm performs its
works and
days

11.9.1990
1.4.2000
© 2012

NOTES TO: BANG THEORY RAG

1   "<u>corpuscular</u> <u>theory</u>, Physics. the theory that light is transmitted
    as a stream of particles. Cf. <u>wave theory</u>"

    "<u>wave theory</u>, Physics. the theory that light is transmitted as a
    wave similar to oscillations in magnetic and electric fields. Also
    called <u>undulatory</u> <u>theory</u>."
                    — <u>Random House Dictionary of the English Language</u>

2   "Eventually they realized that they were in fact detecting a real
    signal from space ... from all directions simultaneously. ... this
    radiation, now called the cosmic background. ... The almost
    inescapable conclusion is that we are in fact observing the faint
    radio 'echo' of the event that created the universe."
                    — A. Fraknoi, "A Faint Echo of the Big Bang",
                            <u>S. F. Examiner and Chronicle</u>, 7.23.78

ABOUT ATMOSPHERE PRESS

Atmosphere Press is an independent, full-service publisher for excellent books in all genres and for all audiences. Learn more about what we do at atmospherepress.com.

We encourage you to check out some of Atmosphere's latest releases, which are available at Amazon.com and via order from your local bookstore:

Melody in Exile, by S.T. Grant

Covenant, by Kate Carter

Near Scattered Praise Lies Our Substantial Endeavor, by Ron Penoyer

Weightless, Woven Words, by Umar Siddiqui

Journeying: Flying, Family, Foraging, by Nicholas Ranson

Lexicon of the Body, by DM Wallace

Controlling Chaos, by Michael Estabrook

Almost a Memoir, by M.C. Rydel

Throwing the Bones, by Caitlin Jackson

Like Fire and Ice, by Eli

Sway, by Tricia Johnson

A Patient Hunger, by Skip Renker

Lies of an Indispensable Nation: Poems About the American Invasions of Iraq and Afghanistan, by Lilvia Soto

The Carcass Undressed, by Linda Eguiliz

Poems That Wrote Me, by Karissa Whitson

Gnostic Triptych, by Elder Gideon

For the Moment, by Charnjit Gill

Battle Cry, by Jennifer Sara Widelitz

I woke up to words today, by Daniella Deutsch

Never Enough, by William Guest

Second Adolescence, by Joe Rolnicki

ABOUT THE AUTHOR

Thanks to his finely skilled teachers and professors at Bishop Loughlin High School, Fordham University and Columbia University Graduate, Michael Zucaro decided to major in English. He deeply enjoyed reading Faulkner, Fitzgerald, Hemingway, Wharton, Shakespeare, John Donne, Virginia Woolf, D.H. Lawrence, and others in depth, fascination, and wonder. He wasn't trying to imitate, but to learn more from them. Enjoying their complexities was vital to him.

His first writing was a short story based on an event a cousin enacted, to which he added an imagined conclusion. Afterward he longed to write other stories, so he jotted bits or fragments, but they began emerging in short lines: the start of poem writing.

Poems evolve from events, often partially complete, but each poem needs to include his speculating why those events happen and what they signify.

CPSIA information can be obtained
at www.ICGtesting.com
Printed in the USA
BVHW070009090223
658148BV00010B/67/J

9 781639 887637